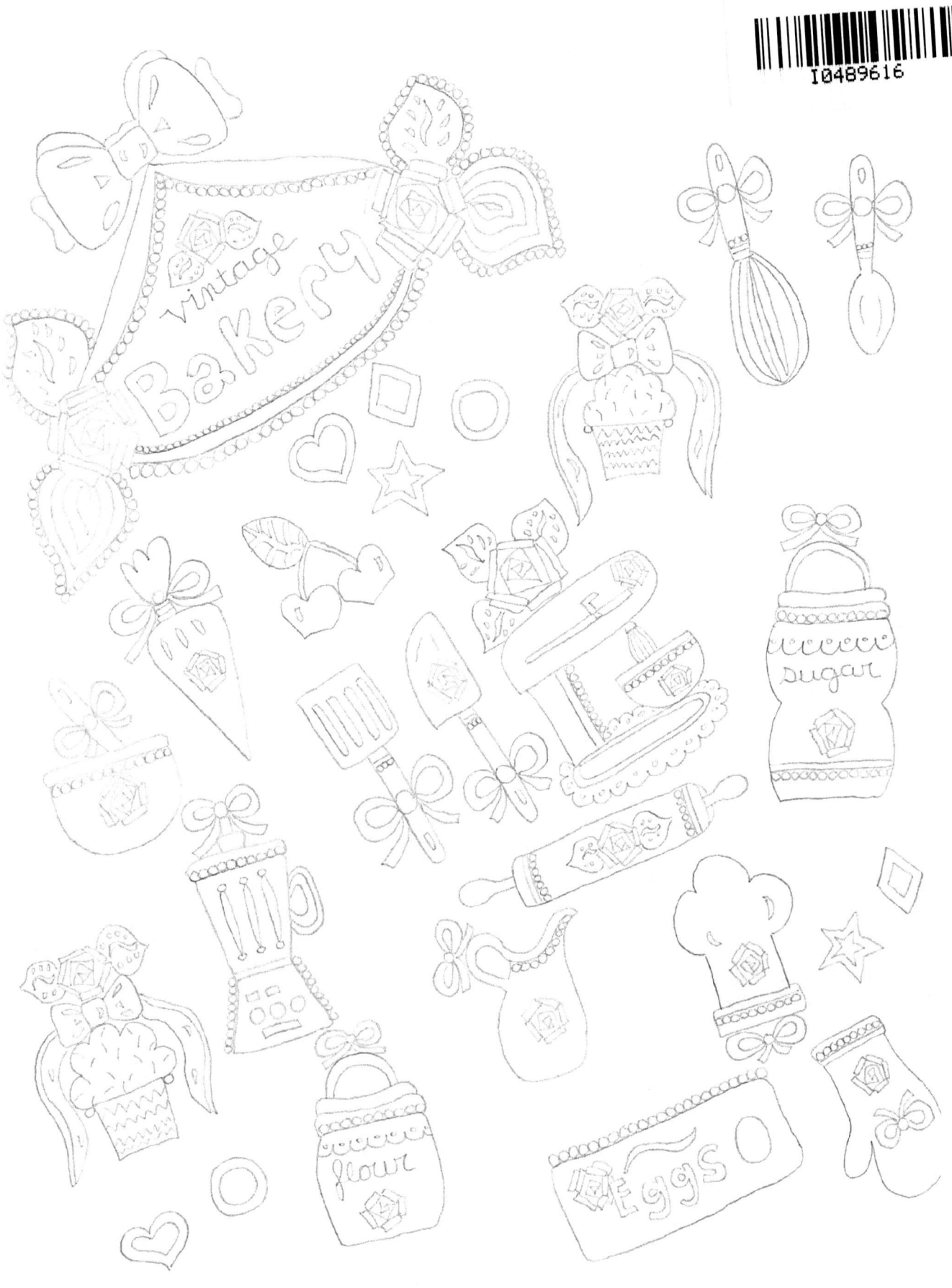

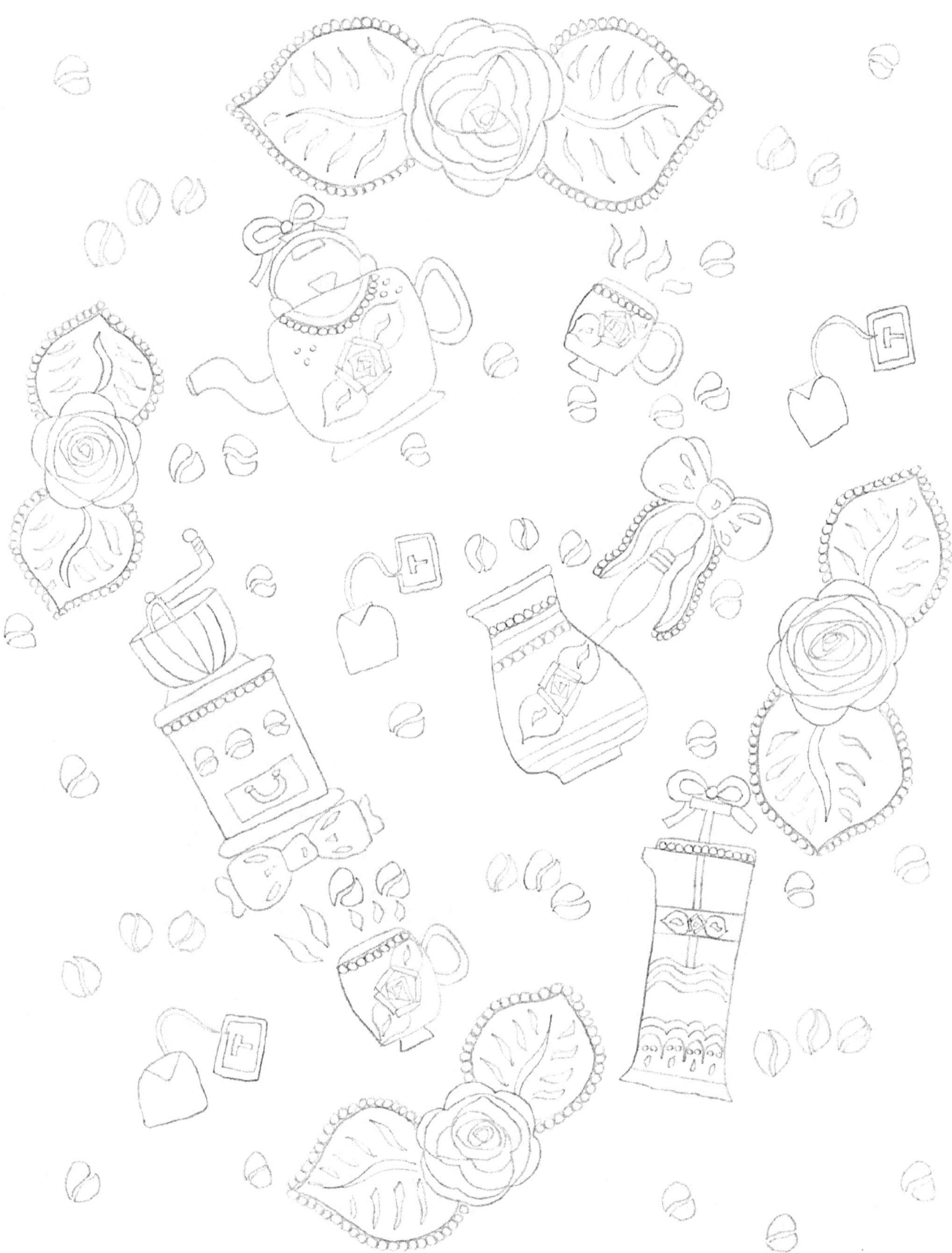

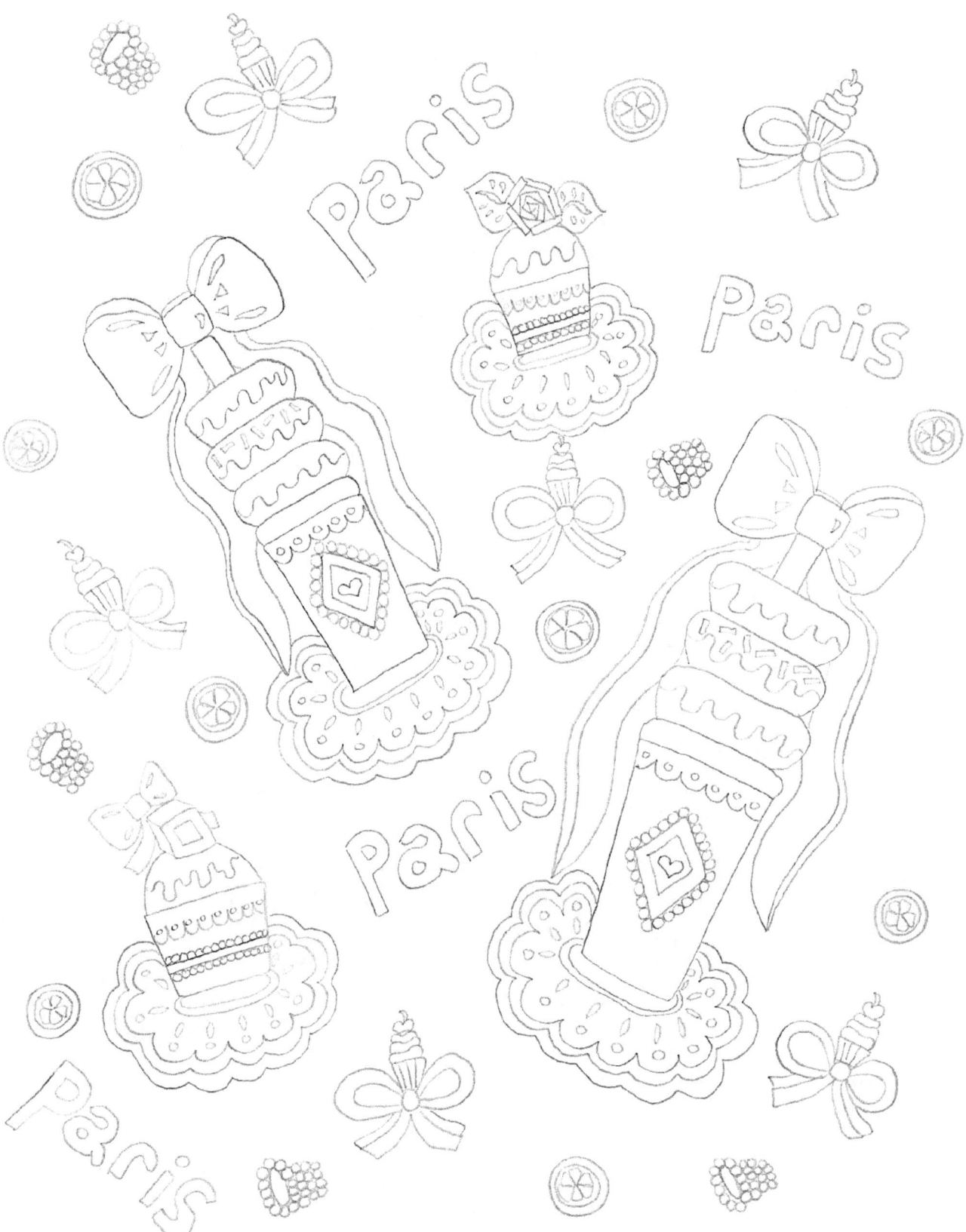

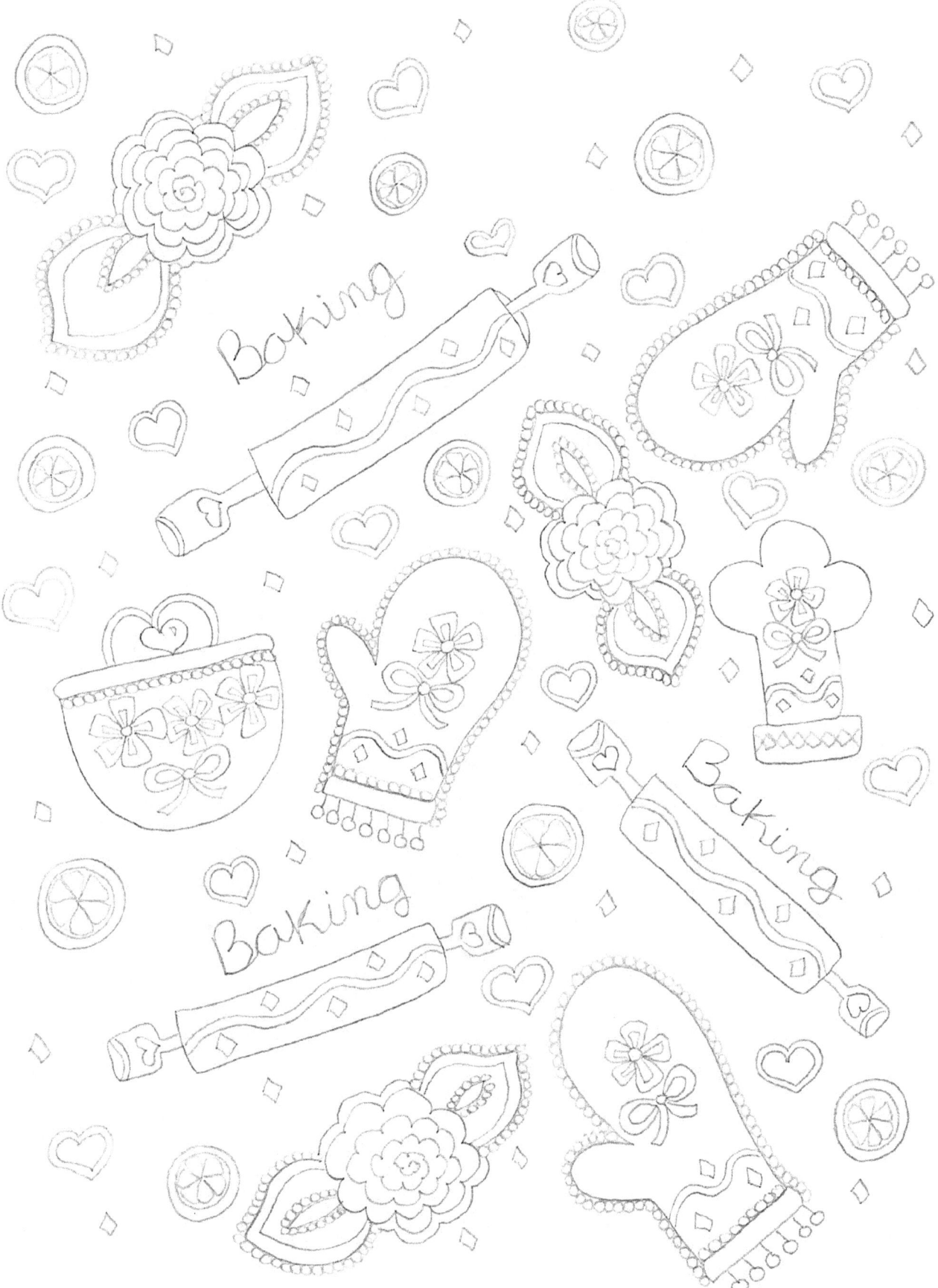

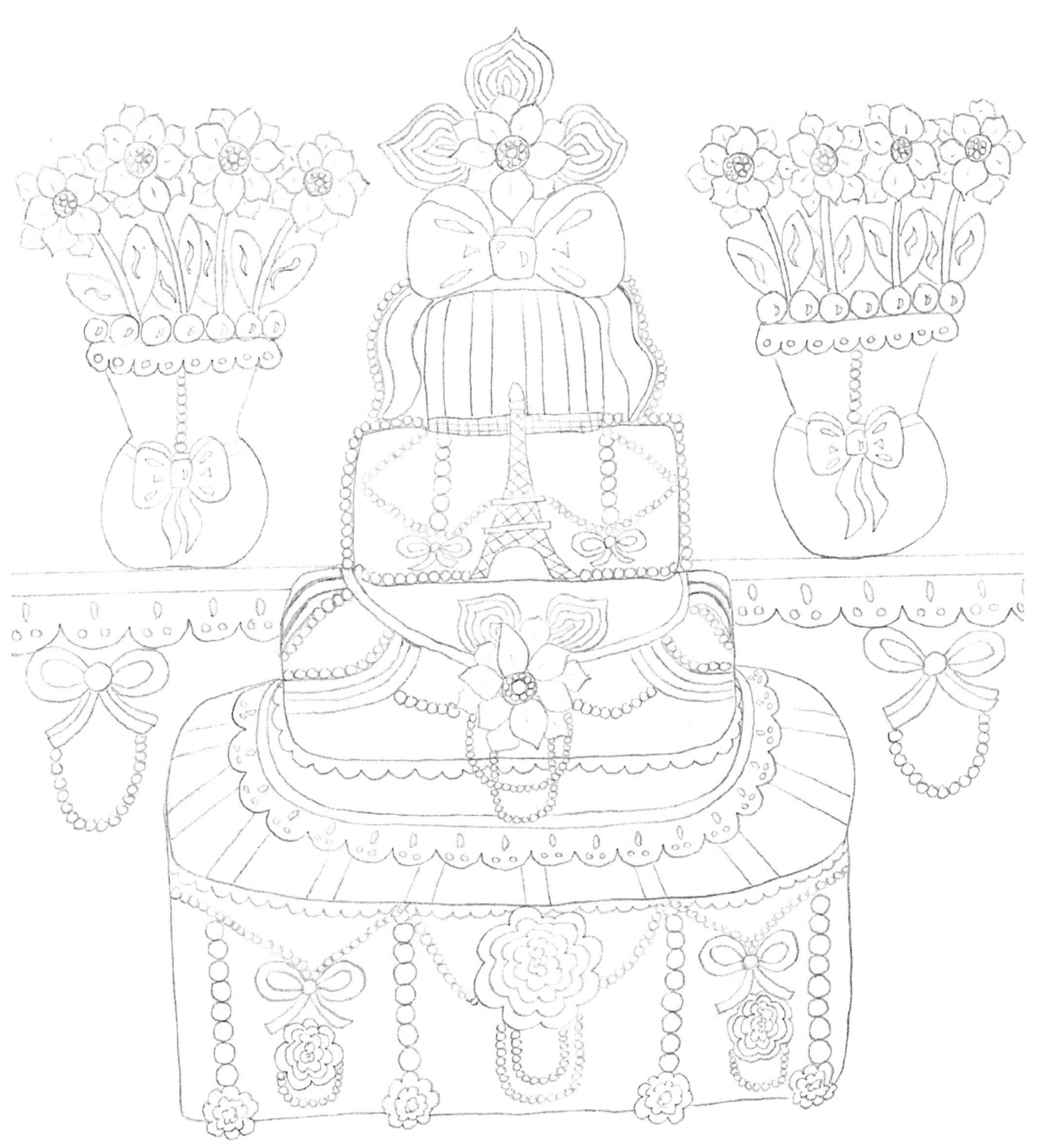

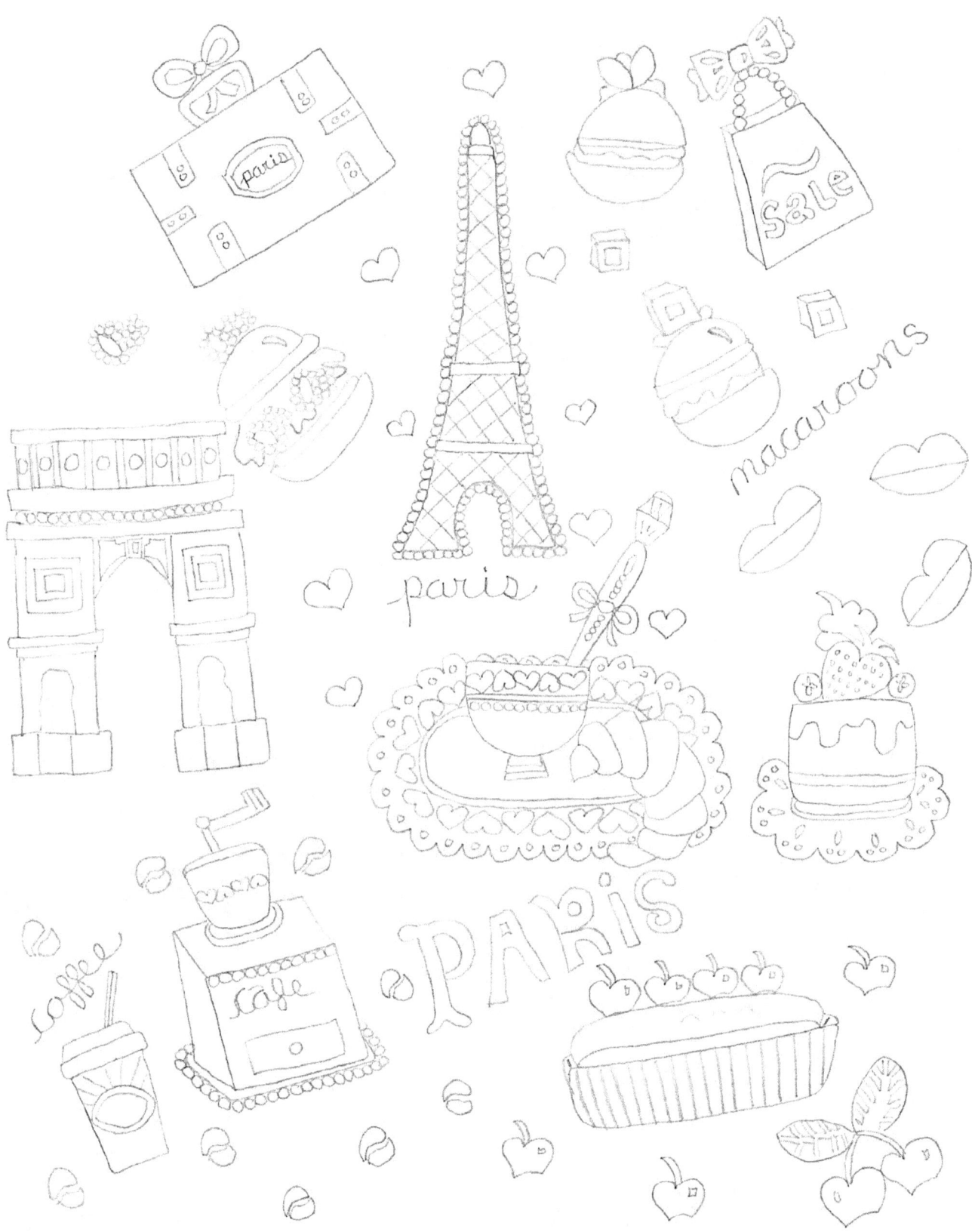

Paris

macaroons

paris

PARIS

café

coffee

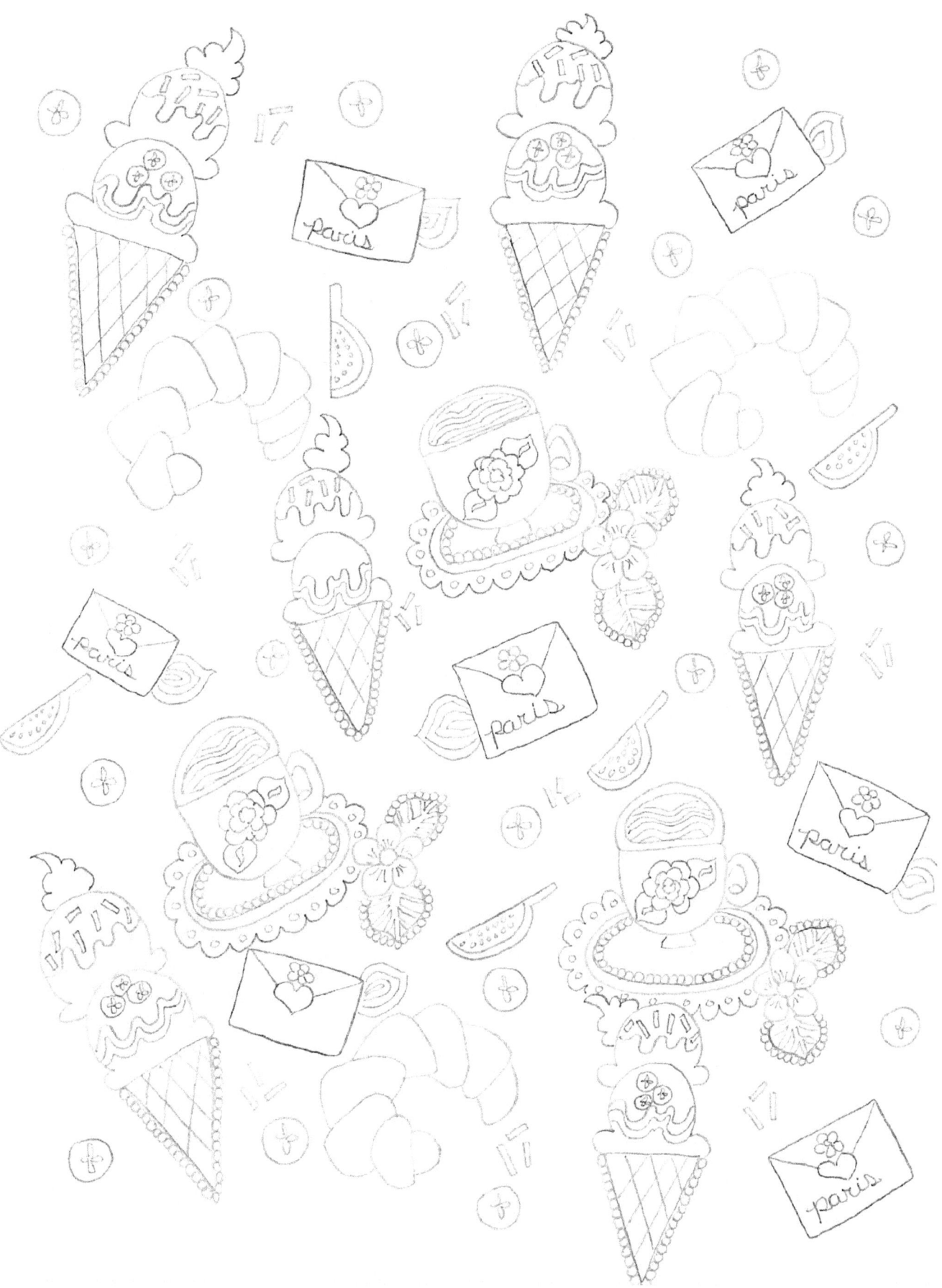

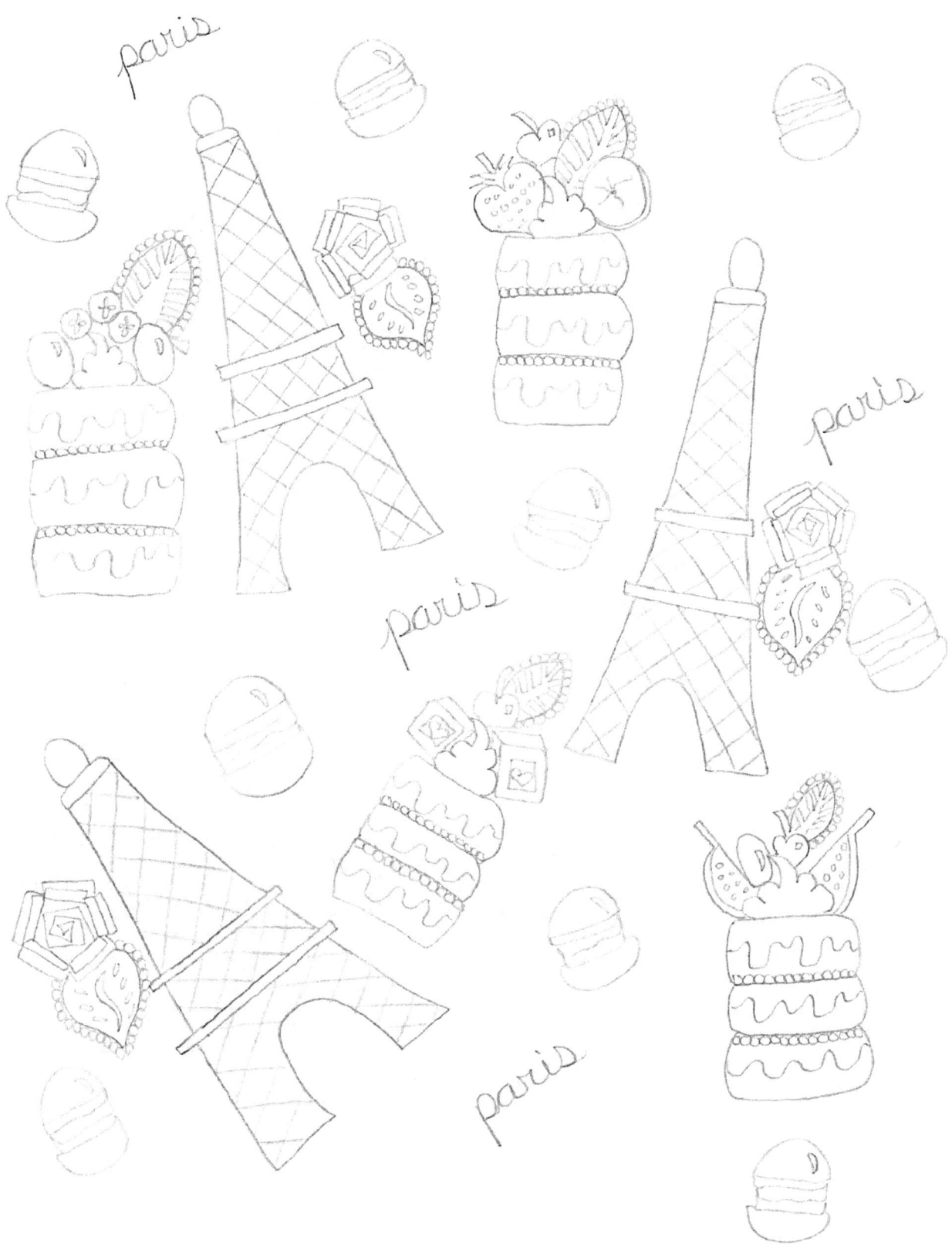

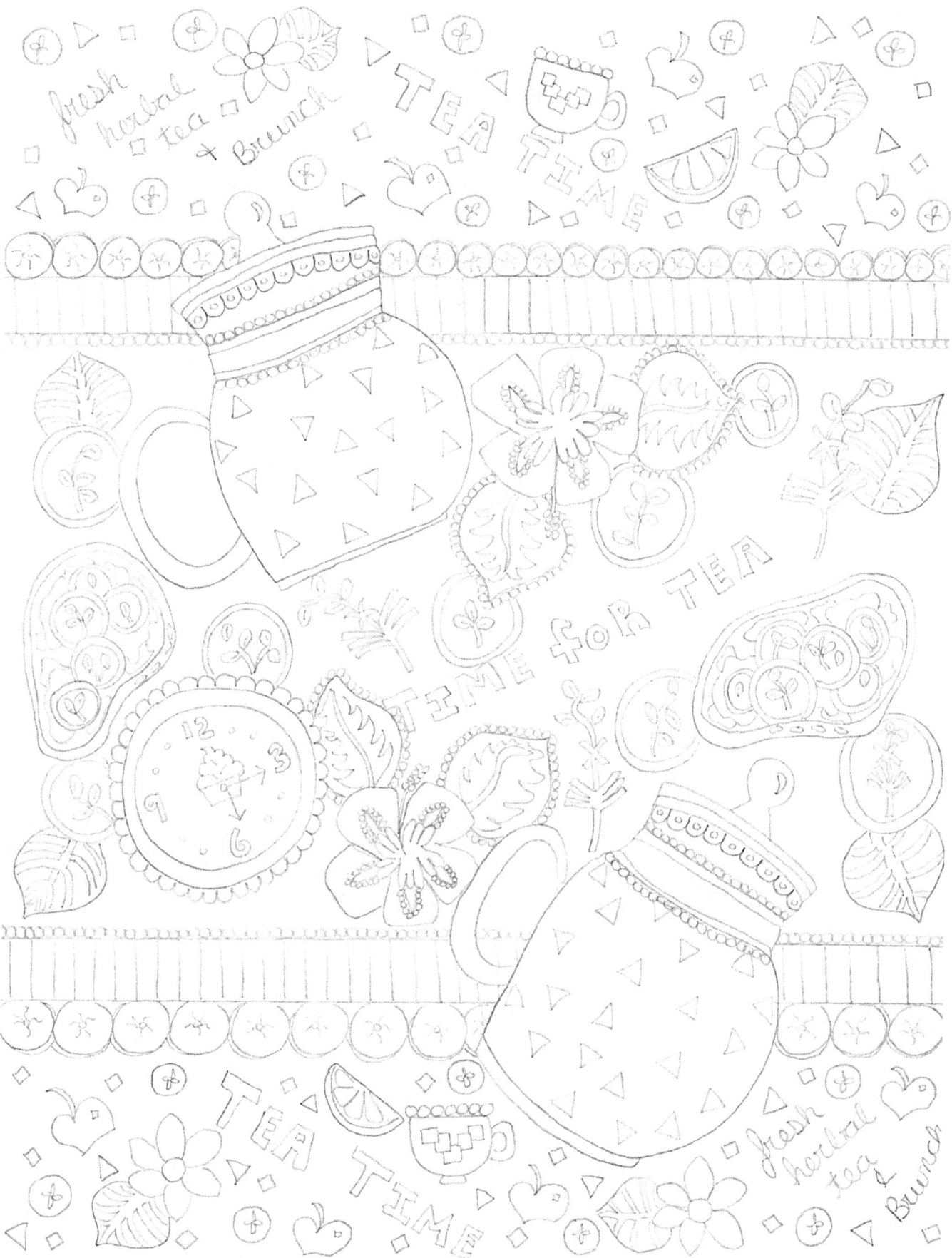

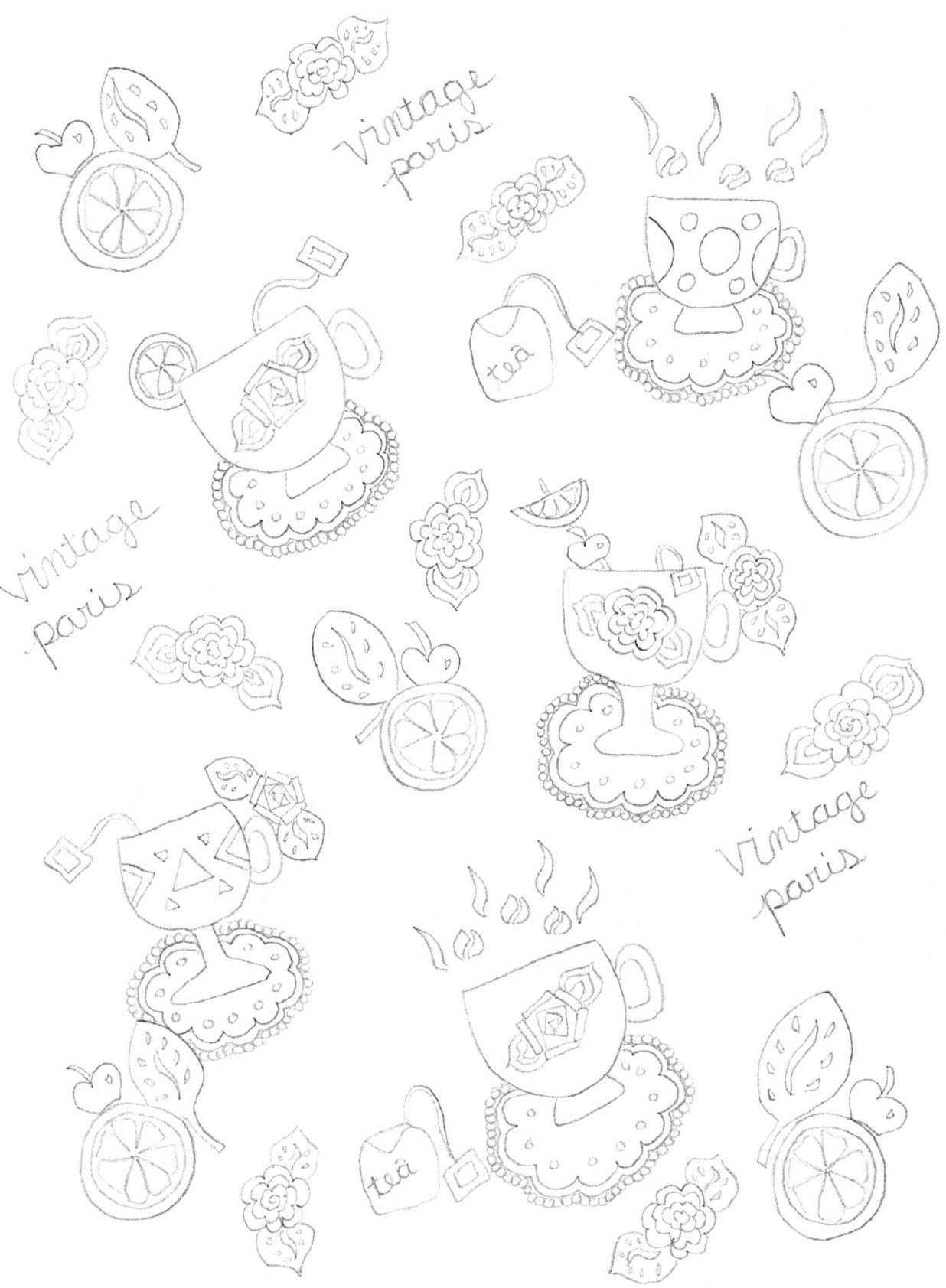

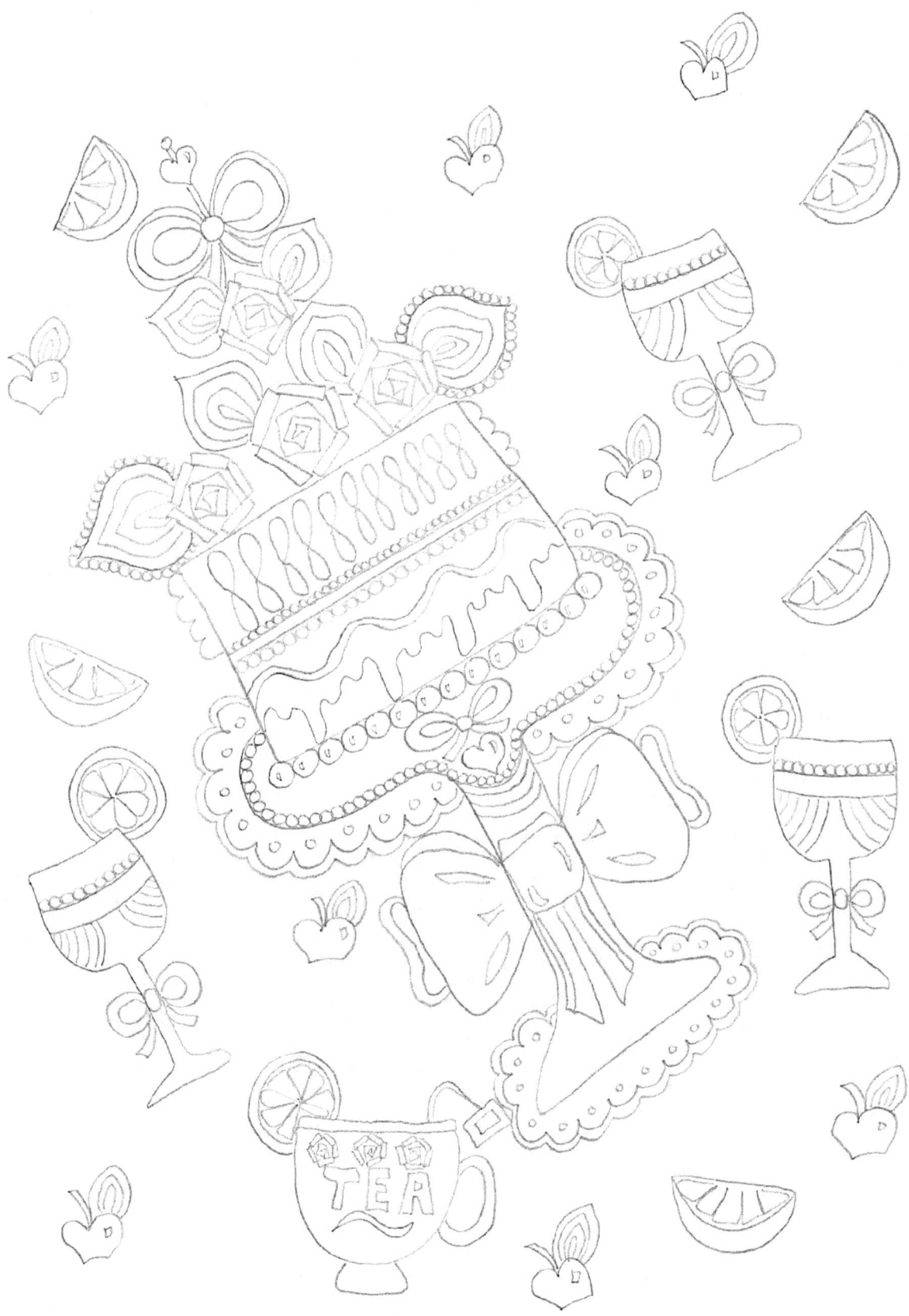

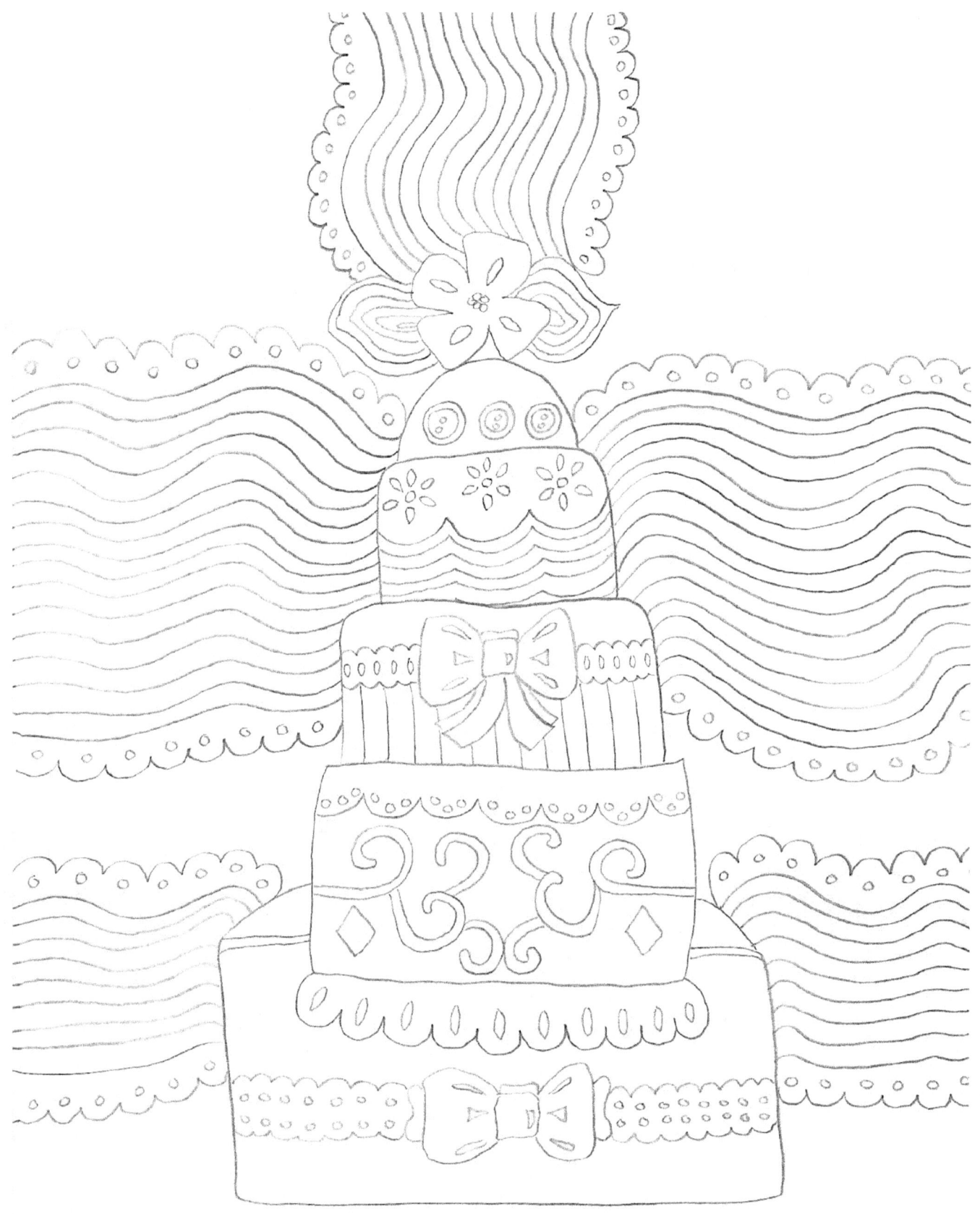

paris - Brest

Dome Cake

friut tart

Apple choux

Éclair

Raspberry
choux

chestnut macaroon
tart

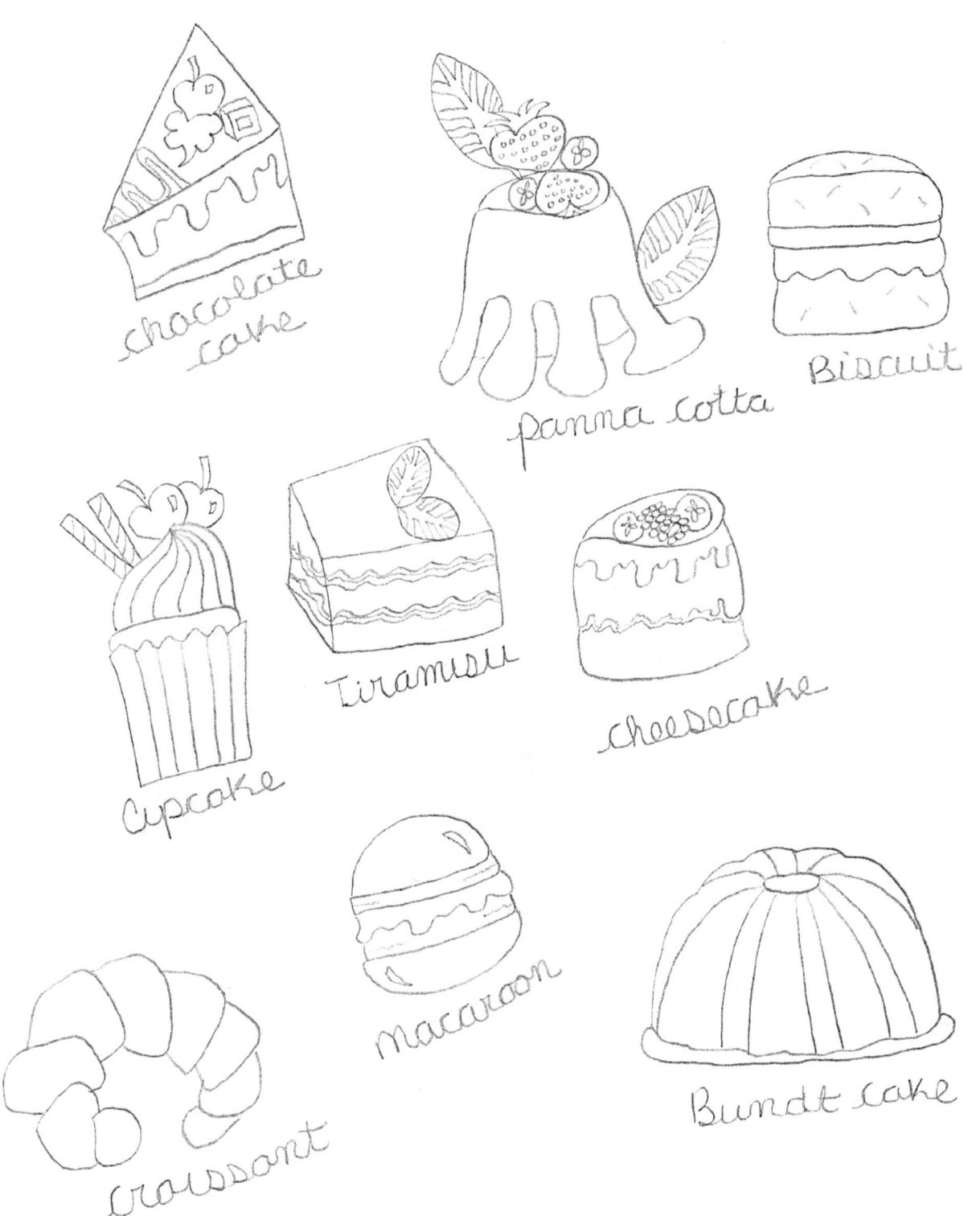

chocolate cake

panna cotta

Biscuit

Cupcake

Tiramisu

cheesecake

croissant

macaroon

Bundt cake

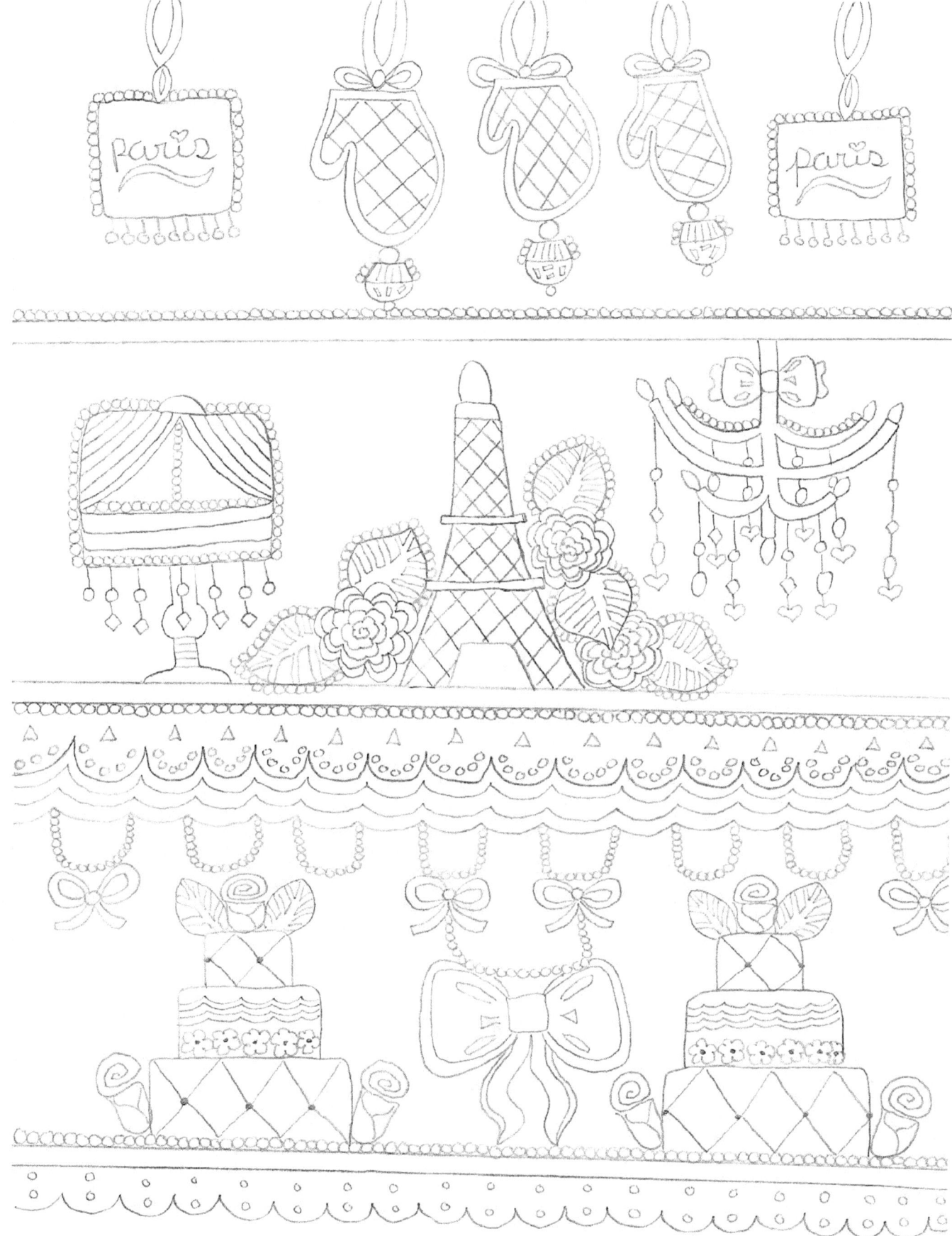

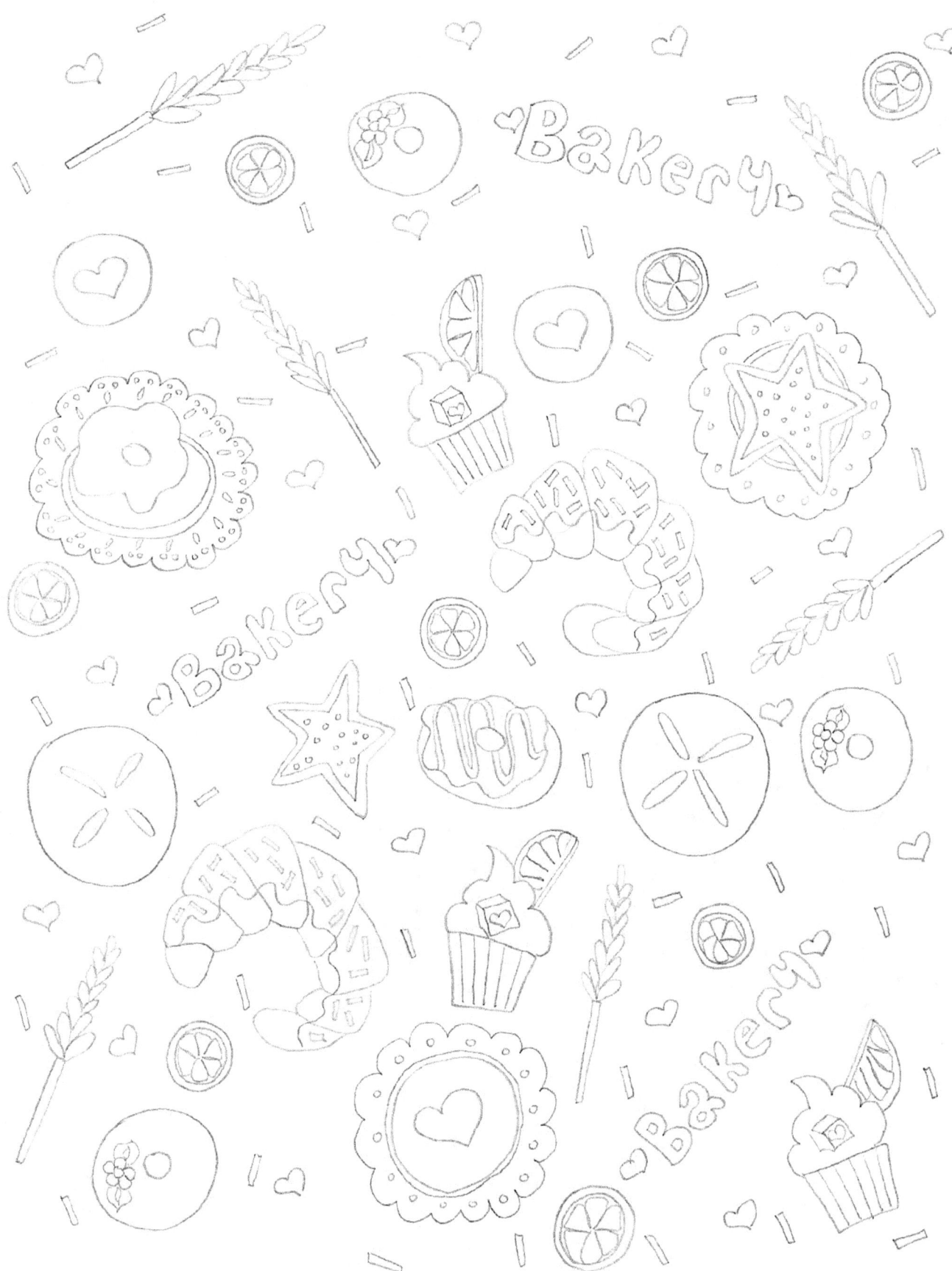

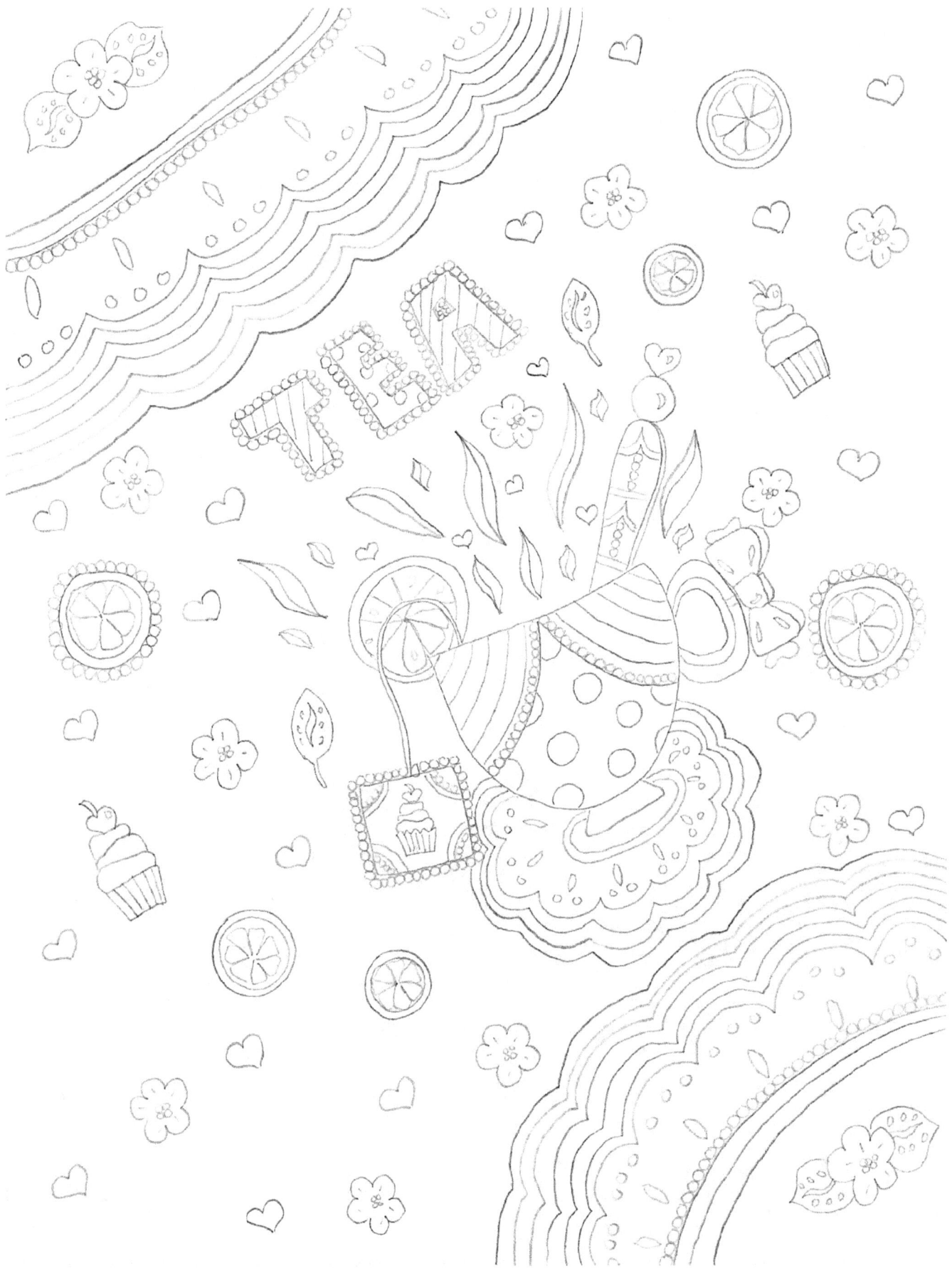